"In a way
practice is like
an
escape
for me.
I can think
about whatever's
on my mind
and I usually
enjoy
practice."

"interviews"

An Interview with
lynne cox

By Gary Libman
Photographs by Dave Cox

CREATIVE EDUCATION/CHILDRENS PRESS

Published by Creative Educational Society, Inc., 123 South Broad Street, Mankato, Minnesota 56001. Copyright © 1977 by Creative Educational Society, Inc. International copyrights reserved in all countries. No part of this book may be reproduced in any form without written permission from the publisher. Printed in the United States.

Library of Congress Cataloging in Publication Data

Libman, Gary.
  Lynne Cox.

SUMMARY: A biography of a young American who is a record-breaking long distance and channel swimmer.
  1. Cox, Lynne—Juvenile literature. 2. Swimmers—United States—Biography—Juvenile literature. [1. Cox, Lynne. 2. Swimmers] I. Title.
GV838.C69L5   797.2′1′0924 [B] [92]   76-42270
ISBN 0-87191-571-5

Lynne Cox had stroked through the frigid, 53-degree waters of the Irish Sea for five hours, covering 13 miles. Suddenly she had to stop swimming, short of her goal, and be pulled into the boat which accompanied her.

"I wasn't feeling," she explained later. "My legs were numb . . . I was so cramped and so cold that I just sort of went into a little ball."

Later Lynne tried to set a world record for crossing California's Catalina Channel. At 11:30 one night she waded into its calm waters and swam strongly for 90 minutes. Then a heavy fog rolled into the Channel, and Lynne sobbed and became hysterical. The swim was over.

"I tried to stop the negative thoughts, tried to keep my mind on swimming by thinking about the books I'd read recently," she told a reporter.

"But I kept thinking about sharks and how far I had to swim . . . The fog may have been partly to blame, but the real problem was that I wasn't ready emotionally."

Lynne later swam the Catalina Channel successfully and set a world record, but cold water and negative thoughts are not the only physical and mental tests Lynne must overcome to be successful in her sport — long-distance and channel swimming.

Long-distance running is difficult, but these races are held in the daytime or under the lights in a stadium. Swimming for distance is often done at night because the tides are generally more favorable during the non-daylight hours. The wind is usually lighter, meaning calmer seas, and there is less boat traffic at night.

However, even at night the tides push the swimmer off course and gigantic waves slap the swimmer in the face. There are also sharks and stinging jellyfish in many ocean waters.

Lynne has wondered, often during a grueling swim itself, whether her accomplishments are worth the effort. Like the marathon runner, the long-distance swimmer is doing it alone. When the water is rough, the boredom is worse because she must concentrate on stroking correctly. She cannot let her mind wander to more pleasant subjects.

Why does a teenage girl subject herself to the

grueling physical and mental torment of long-distance swimming?

"I want to set goals for myself and achieve them. I want to do something a little bit better than anyone else in the world," Lynne says.

Since some of her efforts have taken place in other continents, Lynne has had experiences shared by few other young women. "I enjoy traveling and meeting people," she says.

Family backing also plays a role in her unique unusual sport. Lynne has said that one reason she undertakes her long-distance swims is "because I really have the support of my parents and family."

"I never could have done any of this if it hadn't been for their backing."

Her father, Albert, is a doctor. Neither he nor her mother, Estelle, swim competitively, but they have paid for Lynne's channel swims, which cost about $3,000 each.

Another motivation was that Lynne had not had
great success in regular competitive swimming,
which she was doing until she was 13. "I got tired,"
she said, "of 10- and 11-year-old kids passing me
in the swimming pool."

One day she crossed the Catalina Channel off the
coast of California with three other teenagers.
She kept waiting for them to catch up. The thought
occurred: Maybe this is my thing.

When she was 15, Lynne set a world record of
nine hours and 57 minutes for the 19-mile swim
of the English Channel between England and
France. Two years later, she could approach a
channel swim with confidence, right?

Well, share Lynne's reflections on the beginning of
a world-record swim in the 20-mile Catalina
Channel in 1974:

"I wondered why I was out there and didn't think
I was doing it for myself. But after I thought it
through I wondered — 'Well, who am I doing it for
if not for myself'?"

Though she holds several world-records, Lynne
does not enjoy the satisfaction of performing before

huge crowds. When she began her record-breaking Catalina Channel swim at 10:15 on the night of September 23, 1974, no one had bought a ticket to watch.

As she stepped into the Pacific Ocean, the water temperature was in the low 60's. She was accompanied by a lifeguard paddling a surfboard and a 22-foot boat. The lifeguard was on one side of her, the boat on the other. Her mother and father were in the small boat along with John Sonnichsen, a junior high school physical education teacher who has coached many channel swimmers and is Lynne's advisor and sometime-trainer.

Ahead of them into the dark night moved a 55-foot fishing boat, chartered to watch for possible dangers.

Most of Southern California would be sleeping while Lynne was spending almost nine hours swimming in the ocean. When her hand touched the cliff of Catalina Island at 7:13 the next morning, there was not the applause of thousands to greet her. She merely stepped into the small boat and a record-breaking swim was over.

The new record of eight hours, 48 minutes was two minutes faster than the previous record. That record had been set by her brother, David, two years older than Lynne. He had swum from Catalina Island to Marineland of the Pacific, Palos Verdes Peninsular, and still held that record. Lynne's Catalina Channel record and David's record for men were both broken in late summer of 1976 by other swimmers.

David is Lynne's coach for her channel swims. Often, however, Lynne is alone for her workouts, which may be four to six hours a day. She swims in the ocean almost daily, swimming as far as 15 miles when she's preparing for a channel swim.

Lynne continues her ocean workouts during the school year, when she attends the University of California, Santa Barbara. She also trains with the university's women's team.

When living with her parents at home in Los Alamitos, California, Lynne often works out at a nearby beach in Long Beach. Behind the sand, a row of expensive homes and apartments line the street.

But much of the year the beach is deserted except for a few lifeguards, fishermen, or sun worshippers. There are no sounds save for the crashing of the waves, the infrequent squawk of a sea gull or the occasional distant hum of an automobile engine.

Lynne stood at the water's edge in her swim suit
one fall day, casually inspecting the ocean, ready
for a workout.

"That's a rip," she said, nodding toward a 50-foot
wide area which was colored differently than the
rest of the ocean's surface. Lynne was revealing a
tiny portion of what she has learned from a serious
study of the ocean's behavior, which she began
doing when she became a channel swimmer.

Riptides are dangerous, swirling areas which can
pull a swimmer away from the shore and drown
her if she panics or is inexperienced. "I'll have to
swim around it," she said.

As Lynne talked, a stiff ocean wind bit into the neck
of a fully dressed bystander and chilled him. But
Lynne said she didn't notice the chill. "I'd rather
not weigh as much as I do," she said, "but I think
it helps insulate me and keep me warm." Lynne
weighed 170 pounds. She is 5-feet, 6-inches tall.

Wading slowly into the water, Lynne tugged at an
orange swim cap and tucked in her shoulder
length, blond-brown hair. She dived into a wave to
get wet and stood up again. She swam out about
50 yards, turned right and began stroking parallel
to the shore.

Only her cap, churning arms, and the tip of her ankles were visible as she bored through the water.

Fishermen baited their hooks, sunbathers stared blankly up at the blue sky, and she worked unnoticed.

Finally an elderly woman, walking the shore in a print dress, pointed and said to her companion, "Look, there's somebody swimming out there."

"That's Lynne Cox, the finest distance swimmer in the world," the bystander told her.

"Oh, really," the woman laughed. "No wonder, then," she said and went on.

Meanwhile Lynne kept stroking, one-two, one-two with amazing regularity. Occasionally a wave floated under her and lifted her several feet above the rest of the ocean's surface.

Then about a half-mile down the shore she stopped, reversed direction, treaded water for a few moments and headed back to her starting point. Wading back to the beach, she talked to a few youngsters in shallow water and then came ashore.

Swimming a mile should be a snap for Lynne Cox and practice must be relaxing compared to a channel event? Sometimes. "In a way practice is like an escape for me," Lynne said. "I can think about whatever's on my mind and I usually enjoy practice."

Not always, though, is it enjoyable. "Some days I can't stand to get in the water and I can find reasons for not doing it. But I do.

"When a swim is far off, it really feels good. Then toward the middle of the training period it's hard some days. It's difficult in winter to go into 50-degree water."

Lynne's willingness to put out, to extend herself physically and mentally, goes beyond the swimming itself. Her world record of nine hours and 57 minutes for the English Channel swim from England to France was broken three weeks after it was set on July 20, 1972. An American, David Hart, set a new record of nine hours and 44 minutes. Lynne returned to England in 1973 and recaptured the record, beating Hart's time by eight minutes. Lynne's record was broken twice, once by 33 minutes and again by 40 minutes, in the summer of 1976.

If one effort doesn't accomplish her goal, she comes back another time.

She even tries where others have hesitated. She was the first woman to swim the Cook Strait

between the North and South Islands in New Zealand. Her time for the 13-mile swim in February 1975 was 12 hours and three minutes.

Lynne broke a 50-year-old record for the swim between Vedbaek, Denmark, and Landskrona, Sweden, in the summer of 1976.

On August 16, 1976, she made the first successful swim through the strong currents of the Kattegut Straits. The 15-mile swim from Askedapstander, Norway, to Stromstrad, Sweden, took her six hours and 16 minutes.

Some of the things that motivate this teenage world record holder have been mentioned, but do they keep her going out in the ocean, alone, in the middle of the night?

Starting her record-setting Catalina swim, Lynne knew that getting past the first five miles at low tide, before the high tide began rolling in, would be the most difficult part of the swim.

An hour after she had been in the water, Lynne's determination seemed strong. Stroking powerfully, gulping air on every third stroke, a marker three miles from shore came into view. She was ahead of schedule.

Then Lynne called out.

"I don't want to do this," she said calmly.

"Let's go Lynne," her mother urged. "You've worked all summer, Honey. If you stop now you are going to be very unhappy with yourself. After this you can hang up your suit if you want, but don't let yourself down now."

"Do it like a workout, Lynne," Sonnichsen coaxed. "Everybody I ever knew who swam the channel went through a bad period. You have to work your way through it. Find out how long it takes to get yourself feeling good and find your pace. Use it as a learning experience."

"But I'm not doing it for myself anymore," Lynne replied obstinately. "I'm doing it for everyone else. Mom, I don't want to do it."

"Lynne, we're with you, Honey," Mrs. Cox replied. "We want you to do it for yourself."

Lynne put her head down and started stroking.

Mrs. Cox turned to Sonnichsen.

"I'm afraid she doesn't want to do it. We went through all of this and got it straight with her that she was doing it for herself. I don't want her to think she's doing it for us. I don't understand. It is not like her to be temperamental."

Sonnichsen said all channel swimmers go through periods when they want to stop.

"They want to be told to get into the boat, but if they don't touch the paddler and disqualify themselves, they don't really mean it, and Lynne made no attempt to disqualify herself."

Sonnichsen told the paddler on the surfboard alongside Lynne not to answer Lynne if she talked. But at midnight he asked the paddler if Lynne was lifting her head too fast from the water during her strokes. Lynne heard the question and stopped.

"Damn, why did I talk?" Sonnichsen scolded himself.

A steamer, lights ablaze, glided past in the distance.

"What do you want to do, Honey?" Mrs. Cox asked.

"Lynne, try a feeding," Sonnichsen suggested. "There is a chemical imbalance in your body now, and you can get through it."

"I don't regard myself as a world champion, but as a normal person who has achieved goals I set for myself."

"I don't want to do it for myself," Lynne answered.

"Lynne, the roughest part is over," Sonnichsen urged. "Keep moving. Keep your body moving."

"Come on, Sweetie. C'mon Lynne," Mrs. Cox yelled. "You're the world champion. Don't let your mind tell your body what to do. Keep moving. There's the seven-mile marker out there."

Lynne started stroking again.

At 3:25 in the morning Lynne neared a point called Ship's Rock, seven miles from Catalina Island. Sixty-five minutes later, she asked how many miles she had left and added, "I feel seasick." She was told five or six miles remained.

The sky changed from yellow-gray to pinkish-gray around 6:30 and the sun came up. Lynne was told she had one hour to break her brother's record.

She started swimming hard. When she turned to take a breath, there was a wide grin on her face. She would make it.

The swim through the Cook Strait also required Lynne to persevere when many would quit.

Powerful and unpredictable tides make the Cook Strait one of the most difficult swims in the world. Because New Zealand's two islands form a barrier to ocean currents, water gushes between them, where the swim took place, as through a faucet. Peaks and valleys on the floor of the strait disrupt the cold underwater currents flowing from the Antarctic. The result is countless swirls and eddies.

Northerly winds, gusting up to 45 miles an hour, blew in opposite direction with the tides on the day of Lynne's swim. The winds caused swells up to eight feet. The rough, choppy waters were hard to swim through, quickly tiring the swimmer. Giant breaking waves smashed in her face on whichever side she turned to breathe.

"The waves breaking inconsistently threw off my breathing and my pace," Lynne explained later.

"When you get into a smooth pace it's fun because you can hold it and start thinking about other things. But when you can't get a pace, you have to think about your swimming. That's boring and you can start to feel fatigued . . .

"Several times I was ready to quit. I told myself I could try again when conditions were better," she said.

But she did not quit.

Lynne swam strongly for the first four hours. In the next 90 minutes she stopped to rest five times. After five and one-half hours and well past the halfway point, Lynne stopped once more and stared blankly up toward the small boat beside her. The boat carried Sonnichsen and Lynne's friend, Sandra Blewett, a New Zealand distance swimmer.

"I can't make it," she said quietly. "I want to get out."

Sonnichsen coaxed, then scolded through a bullhorn. When Lynne pulled off her bathing cap and goggles in despair, Sandra shed her sweat suit and leaped into the water.

"Sandy got in and said 'Come on,' and got me going," Lynne said later.

Miss Blewett paced Lynne through swirling waves for an hour until her injured back gave out. She was pulled into the boat, aching and seasick, as Lynne mechanically stroked on.

"It looks like terrible chop out there for miles," the pilot of an escort boat said. "That girl has some kind of guts."

When Lynne's emotions sagged again, more encouragement came.

A New Zealand freighter sailing by in the distance hoisted the American flag in salute.

A New Zealand radio station relayed word to Lynne via her escort boat. She was told that the station's switchboard was jammed with calls from people all over the country, calls urging her to continue.

Yet after two more hours, quitting dominated her thoughts and she needed extra strong encouragement. Then, from nowhere, help came.

For the final four hours of her journey, schools of dolphins arrived periodically to escort Lynne to shore. They came so close to her she could almost touch them. They seemed to smile as they squeaked around her in the water. The last one did not leave her side until she was 35 yards from the finish.

"That was my second major crisis and they got me through it, just like Sandy did the first one," Lynne said later.

"I'd become really depressed and frustrated and within 10 minutes they'd appear and it was like somehow they knew I was trying to get across or they were sent to cheer me up."

Half an hour from the finish a stillness came. The wind suddenly died. A new tide gently tugged Lynne toward the cliffs on New Zealand's South Island.

When she stepped on shore, church bells throughout Wellington, New Zealand's capital, proclaimed her victory over the sea.

It was a rare moment of public acclaim for a young athlete whose efforts are seldom publicly recognized.

Swimming competitively since she was nine, four years after she learned to swim, she may be the best in the world at a sport where most swimmers achieve success only after they're in their 30's.

Not even those closest to her can be sure why she succeeds. Sonnichsen has said that Lynne "gives up all her good times because she has a goal she wants to achieve and she's willing to sacrifice to achieve it."

Lynne agrees with Sonnichsen's observations of her physical abilities. "She is quite large and very powerful in the arms," he says, "so powerful that she needs only a very minimal leg kick."

"She's also willing to accept a pain threshold that the average person wouldn't. And," Sonnichsen observes, "she trains harder or longer than any swimmer I know or have heard of."

Lynne apparently doesn't think that's so impressive. "I don't regard myself as world champion," she says, "but as a normal person who has achieved goals I set for myself."

"My friend, Laura Rothwell, practices the piano four to six hours a day.

"I happen to swim."

creative education

"interviews"